Neighborhood Safari

Foxes

by Dalton Rains

FOCUS READERS

PIONEER

www.focusreaders.com

Focus Readers is distributed by North Star Editions:
sales@northstareditions.com | 888-417-0195

Produced for Focus Readers by Red Line Editorial.

Photographs ©: Shutterstock Images, cover, 1, 4, 6, 8, 10, 12, 14, 17, 18, 21

Library of Congress Cataloging-in-Publication Data
Names: Rains, Dalton, author.
Title: Foxes / by Dalton Rains.
Description: Mendota Heights, MN: Focus Readers, [2025] | Series: Neighborhood safari | Includes index. | Audience: Grades K-1
Identifiers: LCCN 2023050748 (print) | LCCN 2023050749 (ebook) | ISBN 9798889981763 (hardcover) | ISBN 9798889982326 (paperback) | ISBN 9798889983439 (pdf) | ISBN 9798889982883 (ebook)
Subjects: LCSH: Foxes--Juvenile literature.
Classification: LCC QL737.C22 R365 2025 (print) | LCC QL737.C22 (ebook) | DDC 599.775--dc23/eng/20231108
LC record available at https://lccn.loc.gov/2023050748
LC ebook record available at https://lccn.loc.gov/2023050749

Printed in the United States of America
Mankato, MN
082024

About the Author

Dalton Rains is a writer and editor from Minnesota.

Table of Contents

Chapter 1

Sneak Attack

A fox smells a rabbit nearby. It creeps slowly toward its **prey**. Then the fox attacks. It uses its sharp teeth to kill the rabbit. The fox has its meal.

The fox carries its food back to a den and feeds its babies. The den is a hole in the ground. Foxes raise their babies in dens. The den gives the babies a safe place to sleep.

Foxes wrap their tails over their noses to keep warm.

Chapter 2

Body Parts

Foxes are **mammals**. A fox has thick fur and a bushy tail. A fox also has four legs. Each foot has sharp claws. A fox has sharp teeth, too. The teeth can tear through meat.

ear
fur
eye
tooth
tail

A fox has pointed ears. It has a long nose. It also has two eyes. A fox can see well during the day. It can also see well at night.

The smallest foxes can weigh less than 3 pounds (1.4 kg). The biggest can weigh up to 31 pounds (14 kg).

Chapter 3

Hiding and Seeking

Fox fur can be different colors. It depends on where the fox lives. Foxes in cold places may have white fur. Foxes in the desert may have brown fur.

Foxes can be **active** during the day or night. They can see in the dark. That helps them hunt. Foxes have good senses of hearing and smell, too. These senses also help foxes catch prey.

Some foxes can move their claws in and out. The claws help them climb.

Blending In

Red foxes are the most common kind of fox. Their fur is bright. But it acts as **camouflage**. Most of the foxes' **predators** and prey are color-blind. They see green and red as the same color. So, the red foxes' fur blends in with plants.

Chapter 4

A Fox's Life

Foxes **mate** in the winter. Females give birth in dens. Each mother has between 1 and 10 babies. Foxes are blind at birth. They begin to see after about nine days.

Parents care for the **litter** through the summer. By fall, the young foxes are fully grown. They move away from their family. Some will find their own mates. They will have babies the next year.

Foxes usually live alone. They come together only to mate and raise babies.

Life Cycle

Foxes mate in winter.

Females give birth to litters in spring.

Parents care for their litters through summer.

Young foxes move away in fall.

Foxes live alone until it is time to mate.

FOCUS ON

Foxes

Write your answers on a separate piece of paper.

1. Write a sentence describing where foxes live.
2. Would you want a fox to live near your home? Why or why not?
3. When are foxes active?
   A. only during the day
   B. only at night
   C. both at night and during the day
4. Why might foxes in colder places have white fur?
   A. It helps them hide in snow.
   B. White fur is warmer than brown fur.
   C. Colder areas have more trees.

Answer key on page 24.

Glossary

active
Busy or moving.

camouflage
Colors that make an animal difficult to see in the area around it.

litter
A group of babies born to a mother at one time.

mammals
Animals that have hair and feed their babies milk.

mate
To come together to make a baby.

predators
Animals that hunt other animals for food.

prey
Animals that are eaten by other animals.

To Learn More

BOOKS

London, Martha. *Foxes*. Minneapolis: Abdo Publishing, 2021.

Perish, Patrick. *Red Foxes*. Minneapolis: Bellwether Media, 2022.

NOTE TO EDUCATORS

Visit **www.focusreaders.com** to find lesson plans, activities, links, and other resources related to this title.

Index

Answer Key: 1. Answers will vary; **2.** Answers will vary; **3.** C; **4.** A